DIY BARRETTES BOWS & HAIR TIES

BY THE EDITORS OF KLUTZ

KLUTZ

KLUTZ® creates activity books and other great stuff for kids ages 3 to 103. We began our corporate life in 1977 in a garage we shared with a Chevrolet Impala. Although we've outgrown that first office, Klutz galactic headquarters is still staffed entirely by real human beings. For those of you who collect mission statements, here's ours:

CREATE WONDERFUL THINGS • BE GOOD • HAVE FUN

Hair clips, rhinestones, faux leather, glitter fabric, gold letters, and felt made in China. All other components made in Taiwan. 85

Distributed in the UK by
Scholastic UK Ltd
Euston House
24 Eversholt Street
London, NW1 1DB
United Kingdom

Distributed in Canada by
Scholastic Canada Ltd
604 King Street West
Toronto, Ontario
Canada M5V 1E1

Distributed in Australia by
Scholastic Australia Ltd
PO Box 579
Gosford, NSW
Australia 2250

Distributed in Hong Kong by
Scholastic Hong Kong Ltd
Suites 2001-2, Top Glory Tower
262 Gloucester Road
Causeway Bay, Hong Kong

ISBN 978-1-338-64370-1
4 1 5 8 5 7 0 8 8 8

WRITE US
We would love to hear your comments regarding this or any of our books.
KLUTZ
557 Broadway
New York, NY 10012
thefolks@klutz.com

BOX: Font photo ©Tortuga/Shutterstock | CASE: Font photo ©Tortuga/Shutterstock | BOOK: Stock photos ©: cover font: Tortuga/Shutterstock; 7: Maria Shipakina/Shutterstock; 11 top right: cuppuccino/Shutterstock; 11 bottom right: Flamingo Images/Shutterstock

contents

WORD PLAY

Statement Pieces
13

Warm & Fuzzy

Pom-Pom Precious
15

Kitten Cutie
16

Heart of Glitter
19

ICE-CREAM PARLOR

Candy Sprinkles
21

Triple Scoop
22

Cherry Chic
23

Razzle-Dazzle Bow
24

Tropical Charm

Pineapple Puff
27

Twist & Tie
28

Rhinestone Rainbow
29

ACCESSORIZE YOUR VIBE! 30

what you get

Display stand

Faux leather

Black glitter fabric

Paper templates

4 hair clips

Glue

11 pom-poms

60 rhinestones

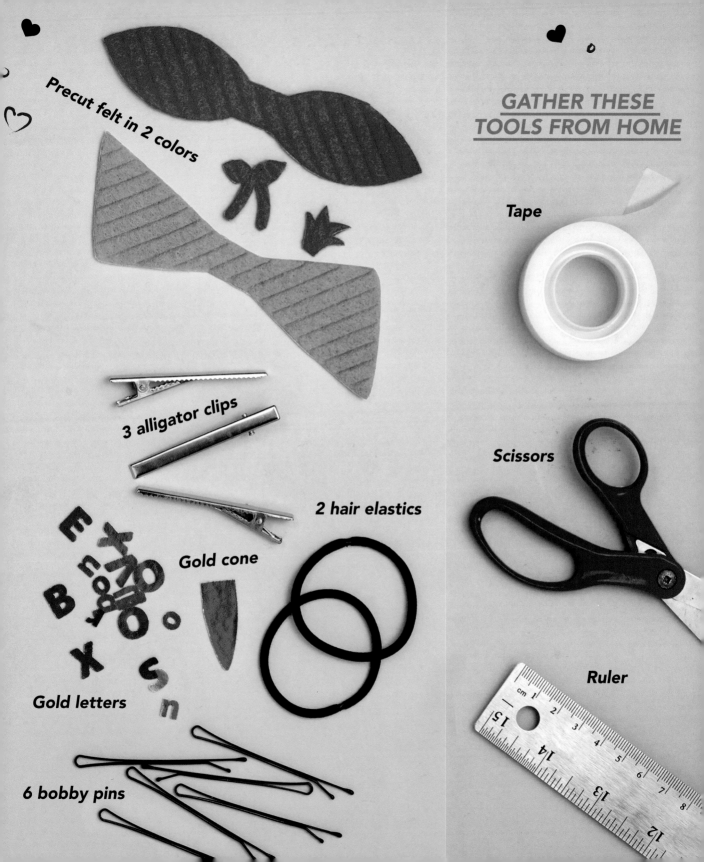

Precut felt in 2 colors

3 alligator clips

Gold letters

Gold cone

2 hair elastics

6 bobby pins

Tape

Scissors

Ruler

make your display

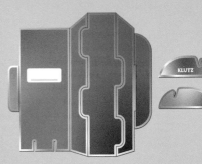

1 Punch out the display design from the cardboard piece.

USE THIS HOLDER WHILE
MAKING YOUR BARRETTES.

2 Fold away from you along the vertical gold lines.

Clip them on to your display when you're done.

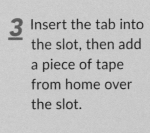

3 Insert the tab into the slot, then add a piece of tape from home over the slot.

 Tip *Punch out the legs and slide them onto the bottom of your stand when you're ready to display your barrettes!*

6

Hair Care

Everyone's hair is different!
Your hair might be curly, fine, straight, coarse, dark, light, or even blue! No matter what your hair is like, it all deserves the same level of love and attention.

A FEW THINGS TO REMEMBER:

✦ *Whether you like to use a comb or a brush, handle your hair delicately. Don't pull your hair tools through tangles or snarls, but instead work them out carefully.*

✦ *Style your hair first. Then add the accessory as the finishing touch.*

✦ *Take your time when you place or remove a hair accessory so it doesn't snag your hair.*

✦ *Your hair might like some help from other products—like styling creams or hair spray—to help ponytails and buns look their best. When in doubt, ask someone you know whose hair looks like yours for advice.*

use your glue

This special paint-on glue is invisible and strong. Make sure to read these tips _before_ beginning your projects.

GLUE PRO TIPS:

+ **PREP YOUR SPACE:** Lay something down to craft on and wash your hands with soap and water if you get glue on them.

+ **LET IT DRY:** The glue needs to FULLY dry in order to work. Make sure to let the glue dry for 1–2 hours before touching your project, and let it dry completely overnight before using your barrette. We know it's boring, but the longer you wait, the longer your barrette will last!

+ **PILE IT ON:** Make sure you paint on a thick coat of glue for your projects. This special glue will dry flat, so don't worry about bubbles. If anything feels insecure, add more glue and let it dry for longer!

+ **CLAMP YOUR STYLE:** Clamping your projects with alligator clips while they are drying makes for a much stronger barrette. Consider making your alligator clips after you've finished your other projects so you can use them as clamps, or use a chip clip or binder clip from home.

+ **CARE AND REPAIR:** Remember that these are homemade, so be gentle with your barrettes once they've completely dried. Keep your extra materials and glue so that if something falls off you can fix it by gluing it back on!

DIY BARRETTES
BOWS & HAIR TIES
GLUE
0.2 fl oz (6 n

Styles for Miles

HERE ARE SOME BASIC STYLES THAT YOU CAN

GLAM UP WITH YOUR NEW GLITTERY ACCESSORIES.

RELAXED BRAID

Separate your hair into three even parts. Loosely cross the right section into the middle. Then cross the left section to the middle. Continue until you get to the bottom of your hair, then tie an elastic. Scrub your braid with flat fingers or gently brush upward with a hairbrush to tease your braid.

TOP KNOT

Separate the top half of your hair, then make a High Bun (page 11). Secure with an elastic. For a relaxed look, gently loosen your bun and tease your hair with your fingers or hairbrush like the Relaxed Braid.

HIGH BUN

Make a ponytail at the crown of your head. Then twist and wrap your hair around to make a bun. Use another hair elastic and bobby pins to secure.

SPACE BUNS

Make a middle part with a comb and separate your hair in half. Make two tight High Buns on either side of your head.

THE SCIENCE OF HAIR

The shape of your hair follicle (the tiny hole in your skin that your hair grows out of) determines the texture of your hair. The more oval-shaped the hair follicle, the curlier the hair. Because each follicle is different, one person may have multiple textures in his or her hair.

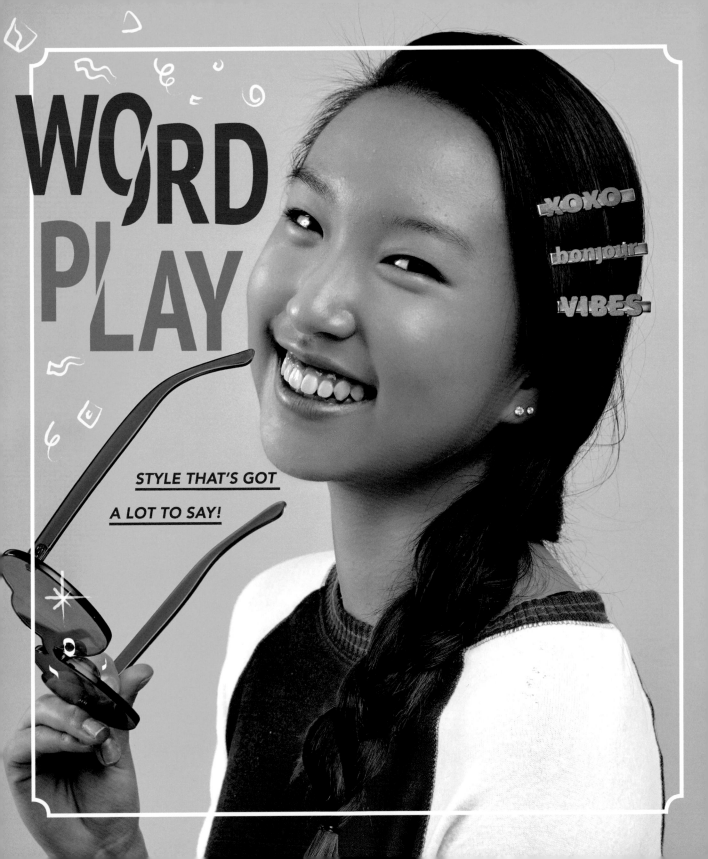

STATEMENT PIECES xoxo

1 Attach your alligator clip to the side of your display stand.

2 Pick out letters for one of the words below, then lay them on the alligator clip to measure spacing.

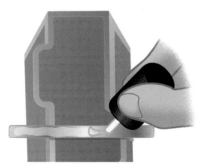

3 Paint a strip of glue onto the front of the clip. Then apply the letters.

4 Let the clip dry overnight.

CHOOSE YOUR WORD   XOXO   bonjour   VIBES

Warm & Fuzzy

YOU KNOW THE FEELING!

Pom-Pom Precious

1 Slide your bobby pin onto your display stand with the long side facing up. Then coat the top of the bobby pin with glue.

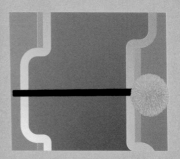

Tip Trim one side of the pom-pom to be slightly flat before adding it to the bobby pin.

2 Press a pom-pom at one end of your bobby pin.

3 Repeat Step 2 to cover your bobby pin with pom-poms, then let the pin dry completely.

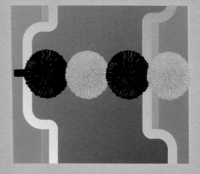

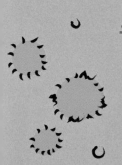

Tip You can clamp the pom-poms with an alligator clip while they dry to keep them in place.

Kitten Cutie

you Will Need

- Bobby pin
- Faux leather
- Glitter fabric
- Kitten Bow, Kitten Ears, Bow Center, and Kitten Whiskers paper templates
- Glue
- Alligator clip (optional)

FROM ❋ Scissors
HOME ❋ Tape

1 Punch out the Kitten Bow paper template, use tape to stick it to the faux leather, and cut out around the paper.

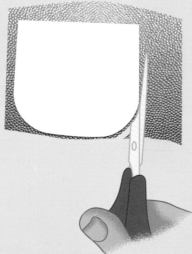

2 Repeat Step 1 to trace and cut the Bow Center, Kitten Whiskers, and Kitten Ears from the black glitter fabric.

Bow Center

Kitten Ears

Kitten Whiskers

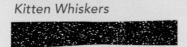

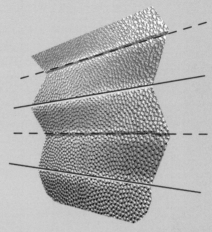

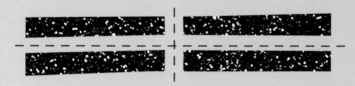

3 Cut the Kitten Whiskers in half lengthwise, then in half widthwise to make four whiskers.

4 Accordion-fold the faux leather back and forth a few times.

5 Pinch the center of the folded leather. It is starting to look like a bow! You can use an alligator clip to help hold it together.

6 Wrap the Bow Center piece around the middle of the folded leather.

* Keep going *

Tip * Use an alligator clip to clamp the pieces together if you are having trouble with the bobby pin. *

7 Dab some glue onto one end of the glitter fabric and hold the ends together by sliding a bobby pin over the spot where the ends overlap.

8 Flip the bow so you are looking at the front. Paint glue on the top two corners of the bow, and place the ear pieces on top.

9 Paint the backs of the whiskers with glue and place two on either side of the center.

10 Let the bow dry overnight, then slide the bobby pin all the way through.

Tip * If you want the bobby pin to be centered on the bow, paint glue on the top of the bobby pin and use an alligator clip to clamp it to the middle back of the bow.

Heart of Glitter

1 Punch out the Hair Clip paper template piece, use tape to stick it to the faux leather, and cut around the paper.

HAIR CLIP

2 Cut a square out of your glitter fabric, about 1 inch wide by 1 inch long (2.5 cm x 2.5 cm).

3 Fold your square in half and cut half of a heart. Unfold the fabric and glue it onto your faux leather piece.

4 Unclip your hair clip and paint glue along the top of the clip.

5 Place the faux leather piece on top of the glue and use an alligator clip to clamp it down in the middle. Let the clip dry completely.

* Tip *

Share the love and make multiple hearts to glue onto your hair clip.

ICE-CREAM PARLOR

MAKE SOME EXTRA

SWEET HAIR CANDY!

CANDY SPRINKLES

You Will Need

- Display stand
- Bobby pin
- 9 rhinestones
- Glue

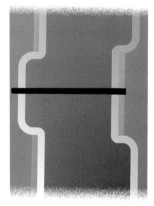

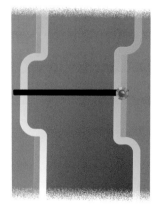

1 Slide your bobby pin onto the display stand and paint a line of glue.

2 Place a rhinestone on top of the glue.

3 Repeat Step 2 to use all 9 rhinestones. Then let the pin dry overnight.

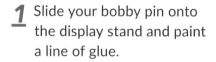

TRIPLE SCOOP

  YUM!

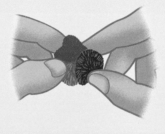

1 Paint glue on the top of each pom-pom. Then squish the glued areas of the pom-poms together to make a triangle.

2 Keep squishing them with your fingers or an alligator clip while they dry completely.

3 Glue the round edge of your hair clip and place the top of the ice cream cone on the glue, perpendicular to the clip.

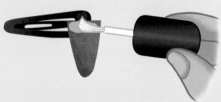

4 Add glue to the top of the gold cone.

5 Place the dried pom-poms on top of the glue and let it dry completely.

tip ✳ If something falls off or doesn't feel securely glued, add more glue, squish the materials together, and clamp it with an alligator clip while you let it dry again!

CHERRY CHIC

you
Will
Need

* Hair clip
* Glitter fabric
* 2 large pom-poms
* Cherry stem felt piece
* Hair Clip paper template
* Glue
* Alligator clip (optional)

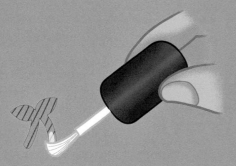

1 Cover the ends of the cherry stem felt piece in glue.

2 Put each end of the stem piece into the top of each pom-pom, then squeeze the pom-pom fluff around the glue.

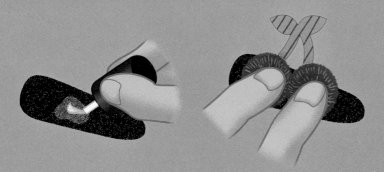

3 Follow Step 1 of Heart of Glitter (page 19) to cut out a Hair Clip shape from glitter fabric. Then paint glue on the center of the glitter fabric and press the cherries on the glue. Let it dry for about 1 hour.

4 Unclip your hair clip and coat the top with glue. Place the glitter fabric on the clip and clamp overnight with an alligator clip like Step 5 of Heart of Glitter (page 19).

RAZZLE-DAZZLE BOW

you Will Need

- Bobby pin
- Faux leather
- Glitter fabric
- Ice-Cream Bow, Ice-Cream Top, and Bow Center paper templates
- Alligator Clip
- Glue

1 Cut out the Ice-Cream Bow and the Bow Center paper template pieces from faux leather (page 16). Place the Ice-Cream Bow piece face-down on your work surface. Paint glue on the middle.

2 Fold one end into the middle, then paint glue on top of the end. Fold the other end on top of the glue and use the alligator clip to clamp the pieces together until they are dry (about 1–2 hours).

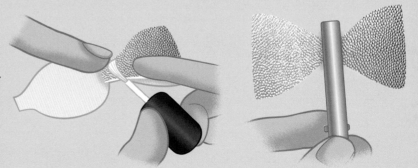

Tip * You can use bobby pins to secure the glitter fabric to the sides of the bow.

3 Cut the Ice-Cream Top paper template out of black glitter fabric and use glue to attach it to the top of the bow, on the opposite side of the end pieces.

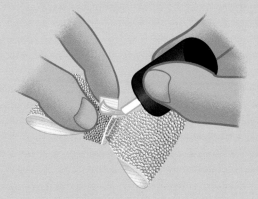

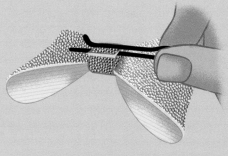

4 Carefully wrap the Bow Center piece of faux leather around the middle of your bow, so the ends overlap on the back side. Use some glue to attach the two ends where they overlap.

5 Use your bobby pin (or alligator clip) to hold the ends together while they dry.

6 Let your bow dry overnight, then slide the bobby pin all the way through.

Tropical Charm

HERE COMES THE FUN.

PINEAPPLE PUFF

* Display stand
* Bobby pin
* Pineapple leaves felt piece
* Yellow pom-pom
* Glue

1 Slide your bobby pin onto the display stand.

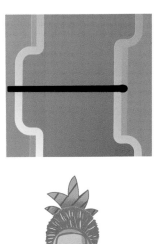

2 Cover the bottom edge of the pineapple leaves with glue and press the pom-pom onto it.

3 Add glue to the end of your bobby pin and press on the pom-pom. Let it dry overnight.

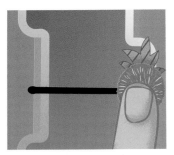

TWIST & TIE

1 Slide the felt piece through the hair elastic so that the elastic is in the center of the felt piece.

2 Fold the wide sections of the felt in half lengthwise, then tie the felt piece around the hair elastic.

3 Pull the felt tight, then straighten out the wide pieces to lie flat.

4 Use your glue to add rhinestones to your hair ties however you'd like. Then let them dry overnight.

RHINESTONE RAINBOW

You Will Need

- Hair clip
- Rainbow paper template
- Glitter fabric
- Pink rhinestones
- Green rhinestones
- Blue rhinestones
- Glue

1 Cut out the Rainbow paper template from the black glitter fabric (page 16).

2 Paint a line of glue along the top edge of the rainbow shape.

3 Place about 12 rhinestones along the edge on top of the glue.

4 Repeat Steps 2–3 for the middle and bottom rows of the rainbow. Then let it dry for 1–2 hours.

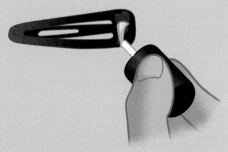

5 Add glue to the rounded edge of your hair clip, then stick the rainbow onto the clip. Let it dry overnight.

Choose your favorite color combo!

accessorize your vibe!

Color Queen

Bow-dacious

Casual Cool

Super
Sweet

So Extra

31

CREDITS

EDITOR: **Kim Rogers**

DESIGNER: **Vanessa Han**

TECHNICAL ILLUSTRATOR: **Kat Uno**

DOODLE ILLUSTRATOR: **Reese Walker**

PHOTOGRAPHER: **Biz Jones**

GROOMER: **Daniella Shachter**

MODELS: **Juliet, Jay, Sam, Owen Keating, and Dana Kaminsky**

BUYERS: **Mimi Oey and Sam Walker**

PACKAGE DESIGNER: **Owen Keating**

PRODUCT DEVELOPMENT MANAGER: **Gina Kim**

SAFETY MANAGERS: **Sam Walker and Karen Fuchs**

SPECIAL THANKS: **Stacy Lellos, Netta Rabin, Caitlin Harpin, Meghan Marin, and Hannah Rogge**

Get creative with more from KLUTZ

Looking for more goof-proof activities, sneak peeks, and giveaways? Find us online!

KlutzCertified KlutzCertified KlutzCertified KlutzCertified Klutz

Klutz.com • thefolks@klutz.com • 1-800-737-4123